MOUNTAINS

ENDANGERED
BIOMES

DONNA LATHAM

Printed by Regal Printing Limited in China,
June 2011, Job Number 1105033
ISBN: 978-1-936313-53-2

Educational Consultant, Marla Conn

Questions regarding the ordering of this book should be addressed to
Independent Publishers Group
814 N. Franklin St.
Chicago, IL 60610
www.ipgbook.com

Nomad Press
2456 Christian St.
White River Junction, VT 05001
www.nomadpress.net

Image Credits

Corbisimages.com/ Paul Souders, cover; Stringer/Indonesia/Reuters/Corbis, 20.

©iStockphoto.com/ Gregory Olsen, title pg, 25; Jussi Santaniemi, 1; Jay
Rysavy, 1; Nicholas Roemmelt, 3; Ooyoo, 5; Rusm, 6; Ken Canning, 7; Max
Popov, Masek, 9; Scott Cramer, Adventure Photo, 9; BasieB, 9; Zennie, 9;
FotoVoyager, 10; Andipantz, 11; KingWu, Kings Photo, 12; Schmitz Olaf,
12; Paul Prescott, 13; Eric Isselée, Life on White, 14, 15; Technotr, 15;
Marcus Lindström, Moonshadow Media, 16; Caroline Vancoillie, 16; Niko
Guido, 18; Jon Faulknor, 18; Sondra Paulson, 19, 22; Giorgio Fochesato,
21; S. Greg Panosian, 23; Carmen Martínez Banús, Maica, 26.

CONTENTS

What Is a Biome?

Grab your backpack! You're about to embark on an exciting expedition to explore one of Earth's major **biomes**: the mountains!

A biome is a large natural area with a distinctive **climate** and **geology**. The desert is a biome. The ocean, grasslands, and tundra are biomes. So are mountains.

Did You Know?

Scientists don't agree on how many biomes there are. Some divide the earth into five biomes. Others argue for 12.

biome: a large natural area with a distinctive climate, geology, and set of water resources. A biome's plants and animals are adapted for life there.

climate: average weather patterns in an area over many years.

geology: the rocks, minerals, and physical structure of an area.

biodiversity: the range of living things in an ecosystem.

adapt: changes a plant or animal makes to survive in new or different conditions.

ecosystem: a community of living and nonliving things and their environment. Living things are plants, animals and insects. Nonliving things are soil, rocks, and water.

environment: everything in nature, living and nonliving.

Each biome has its own **biodiversity**, which is the range of living things **adapted** for life there. It also contains many **ecosystems**. In an ecosystem, living and nonliving things interact with their **environment**.

Teamwork keeps the system balanced and working. Earth's biomes are connected together, creating a vast web of life.

2

Landscape and Climate

Mountains soar high over every continent.
They cover 20 percent of the earth's land surface.
Mountains are usually found in groups called
chains or ranges, though some stand alone. Ranges
in the mountain biome include the Rockies, Sierra
Nevada, and Cascade Mountains in North America.

**The Andes in South America,
the Himalayas in Asia, the Alps
and Pyrenees in Europe, and
the mountains of the Great
Rift Valley in Africa are also
part of the mountain biome.**

of the Mountains

deciduous forest: a forest where most trees and bushes shed their leaves at the end of the growing season.

coniferous forest: a forest where most trees and bushes produce their seeds in cones and do not lose their leaves each year. Many have needles for leaves.

treeline: as far up a mountain as trees can grow.

tundra: a vast region in the Arctic without trees. The soil below the top layer is always frozen.

As you climb a mountain, you travel through many biomes. The lower slopes of mountains often have waving grasslands or vast deserts. **Deciduous forests** can sprawl at a mountain's foothills.

Keep climbing, and you'll move through **coniferous forests** that cover mountains in lush green. Higher up above **treeline**, mountain peaks are snow covered in winter and sometimes all year. It's like the **tundra** here!

Rainfall varies greatly across the world's mountains. Some are very wet and some are very dry—and some are in between!

The mountain biome is cold and windy. The higher the **altitude**, the colder and windier it gets. Summer temperatures can be chilly, averaging from 50 to 59 degrees Fahrenheit (10 to 15 degrees Celsius). Winter can last from October to May. Temperatures stay below freezing and plunge to -40 degrees Fahrenheit or colder (-40 degrees Celsius).

Andean condor

Did You Know?

It takes thousands of years for a waterfall to form. Flowing water wears away at the land little by little. Sometimes it gets down to a rocky area that doesn't wear away from **erosion**. Frothy waters tumble over rocky ledges and into streams or rivers below.

Weather in the mountains changes quickly. In minutes a thunderstorm or snowstorm can roll in when the sky was perfectly clear. Temperatures can quickly drop from pleasant to below freezing.

Words to Know

altitude: the elevation, or the height above sea level or the earth's surface.

erosion: when land is worn away by wind or water.

6

Mountain ranges have formed through **geological events** over millions of years. The earth's crust is made of huge **plates** that drift. An earthquake happens when these plates crash into one another. The pressure causes some land to sink. Other land lifts and folds. Some mountains are volcanoes that form when melted rock surges through cracks in the earth's crust.

Over time, erosion by glaciers, water, and wind carve mountain landscapes.

Word Exploration

Krummholz trees are stunted, twisted trees that grow just above the treeline. *Krummholz* comes from the German words *krumm*, which means "twisted," and *Holz*, for "wood."

Words to Know

geological events: earthquakes, eruptions of volcanoes, and erosion.

plates: huge moving pieces of the earth's crust.

glacier: an enormous mass of frozen snow and ice that moves across the earth's surface.

Plants Growing in the

You'll encounter different life zones on mountains. Life zones describe **ecological communities** and where they are located on mountains. Different plants and animals are adapted for life in each life zone.

In North America's Rocky Mountains, the three main life zones are montane, subalpine, and **alpine**. The montane level is located at altitudes up to 8,000 feet above sea level (2,438 meters). It's the warmest and driest zone and the nicest for people and wildlife.

Douglas fir

Aspen

Blue spruce

Lodgepole pine

Mountains Have Adapted

Words to Know

ecological community: the relationship between living things and their environment.

alpine: relating to mountains.

Aspen trees, blue spruce, Douglas firs, and lodgepole pines are common in the montane zone.

The subalpine zone lies at altitudes between 8,000 and 11,500 feet above sea level (2,438 to 3,505 meters). The trees here—mostly firs and spruces—are shorter and more scattered.

Above 11,500 feet (3,505 meters) is the alpine zone. Here above the treeline, wildflowers and shrubs have adapted by growing close to the ground to stay out of the wind. High winds and a short growing season make conditions difficult.

How difficult are growing conditions high in the mountains?

Powerful winds prevent trees from growing upright. They lurch sideways and look more like shrubs than trees.

Words to Know

habitat: a plant or animal's home.

perennials: plants that live for more than one season.

annuals: plants that flower and die in one season. New plants grow the next year from seeds.

succulent: a plant with thick leaves that can store water.

To survive in the harsh mountain **habitat**, alpine plants are **perennials**. They don't have to use their precious energy to grow roots, stems, and leaves in one season, the way **annuals** do. As soon as spring arrives they can grow their leaves. And many high mountain plants are **succulents** that store water in thick leaves.

Scattered spruce trees have branches and needles on one side, like a flag. This is called flagging. It is a result of winds that constantly push on the trees.

Animals Living in the

The yak is a shaggy member of the ox family that lives in Asia's Himalayas. Its big chest with huge lungs allows it to inhale large amounts of air. A fleecy outer coat and a downy inner one provide a double layer of protection against the bitter cold.

What Eats What?

Herbivores at the bottom of the **food chain** eat grass and other plants. Grass-eating Himalayan marmots are nicknamed "whistle pigs" because they whistle shrilly to alert each other when they spot a **predator**. Snow leopards at the top of the food chain are **carnivores** that eat marmots and other **prey**, such as ibex and wild sheep. The Tibetan wolf preys on yaks.

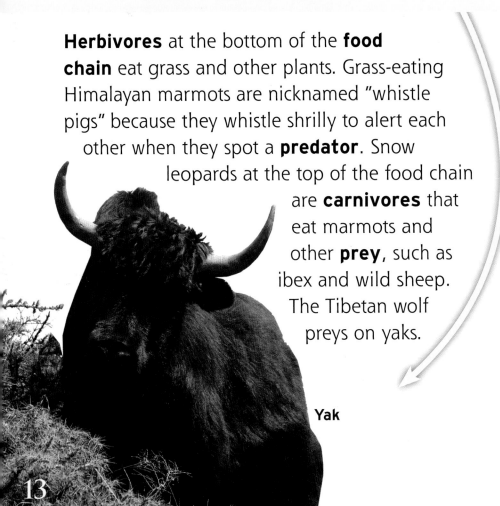

Yak

Mountains Have Adapted

Did You Know?
The higher the altitude, the less oxygen in the air. The low level of oxygen can make you feel dizzy.

Llama

Llamas roam all over the tricky mountain terrain of the Andes of Peru. Their double-toed feet with leathery bottom pads keep them from stumbling. Like the yak, llamas have a thick coat. They also have large lungs to help them get the oxygen they need.

Words to Know

herbivore: an animal that eats only plants.

food chain: a community of animals and plants where each is eaten by another higher up in the chain.

predator: an animal that hunts another animal for food.

carnivore: an animal that eats only other animals.

prey: an animal hunted by a predator for food.

An oily coating covers the giant panda's woolly fur. This adaptation is like a waterproof raincoat that keeps the panda warm in China's mountains.

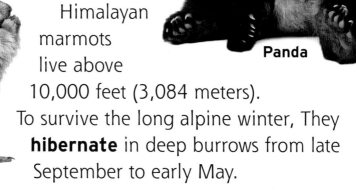
Panda

Marmot

Himalayan marmots live above 10,000 feet (3,084 meters). To survive the long alpine winter, They **hibernate** in deep burrows from late September to early May.

Ibex

Snow leopards

Pine marten

here: The pine marten of the Rocky Mountains sprouts extra fur on its toe pads to keep its feet toasty as it scurries over snow. This extra fur turns their feet into little snowshoes to help them stay on top of the snow.

there: The desert's fennec fox also grows thick fur on its feet. This extra fur shields the fox's feet from the scorching sands of the desert.

Environmental Threats

Natural events including landslides and brushfires impact fragile mountain ecosystems.

Habitat destruction from human activities such as constructing ski areas, mining, logging, and farming all pose threats to mountain regions. Each contributes to habitat destruction as more land is cleared.

Global warming may be the biggest threat. As warmer temperatures melt glaciers, ecosystems are changed forever. At each life zone, mountain animals must **migrate** to new habitats, often in higher areas.

Acid rain comes from burning fuels like coal, heating oil, and gasoline. This polluted rain slows growth in trees at high altitudes by damaging their leaves. It has killed off many fish **species** in mountain lakes.

Words to Know

migrate: to move from one environment to another when seasons or conditions change.

species: a type of animal or plant.

Biodiversity at Risk

As more and more mountain habitat is destroyed, animals are forced to move. A mountain's shape can cause a problem. Once animals settle high at the top, there's nowhere left to move.

In China, pandas are a symbol of peace. They're also the symbol of the World Wildlife Fund. Sadly, the giant panda is almost **extinct**. People have cleared away the panda's habitat to provide logs for fuel and land for rice farms. They have chopped down the bamboo plants that pandas eat. Searching for bamboo, pandas have moved to distant mountains in southern China.

The 2-ounce pygmy tarsier can fit in the palm of your hand.

Pygmy tarsier

With its oversized eyes and ears, this teeny animal can swivel its head 180 degrees like an owl. Scientists believed the pygmy tarsier became extinct in 1921. Then in 2008 they were amazed to find four tarsiers in the mountains of Indonesia. Scientists think that the pygmy tarsier suffered when logging cleared away its habitat.

Words to Know

extinct: the species has completely died out. It has disappeared from the planet.

Path to Extinction

Rare: Only a small number of the species is alive. Scientists are concerned about the future of the species.

Threatened: The species lives, but its numbers will likely continue to decline. It will probably become endangered.

Endangered: The species is in danger of extinction in the very near future.

Extinct in the Wild: Some members of the species live, but only in protected captivity and not out in the wild.

Extinct: The species has completely died out. It has disappeared from the planet.

The Future of the

Climate change is a major threat to mountain ecosystems. As earth's temperatures rise, glaciers in mountain regions melt. What happens in one biome has an effect on other biomes as well. The World Wildlife Fund reports that melting glaciers could result in floods in some areas and water shortages in other areas. The rise in sea level will threaten and destroy coastal communities and habitats.

At great risk is Mt. Kilimanjaro, the highest peak in Africa. The Furtwangler Glacier on Kilimanjaro shrank by 50 percent between 2000 and 2009.

Mountains

About 80 percent of our planet's freshwater comes from the mountains. Half of the world's people depend on mountains for freshwater. So it is important to protect the mountain biome.

In the Andes of South America, glaciers are already disappearing. People in Bolivia, Ecuador, and Peru depend on these glaciers for their water supplies. They create electricity from powerful rivers that start in their mountains.

People are increasingly aware of the delicate balance of life on Earth. Many are devoted to conserving nature and preserving our biomes.

Conservation Challenge

Think about what You can do to benefit the environment. What actions can you take? How can you inspire others to do the same?

Start by saving water. When washing dishes by hand, don't let the water run while rinsing. Use your clothes washer and dishwasher only when they are full, and cut back on watering your lawn. If you shorten your shower by a minute or two, you'll save up to 150 gallons of water a month.

Pick up Trash. Fill an extra collection bag when you go shell hunting or rock collecting.

Pick up bottle caps, plastic bags, and other litter.

Mountain goat

25

Reuse. Pack waste-free lunches. Use a lunch box or tote. Instead of disposable utensils, pack reusable ones. Instead of single-serving juice bags or bottled water, pour your drink into a thermos. Compost leftover food scraps.

Garden. Grow your own food. Pitch in at a community garden, or transform a section of your yard. Plant veggies, herbs, and fruit bushes. Share your harvest with friends and neighbors and arrange a seed swap.

Glossary

adapt: changes a plant or animal makes to survive in new or different conditions.

alpine: relating to mountains.

altitude: the elevation, or the height above sea level or the earth's surface.

annuals: plants that flower and die in one season. New plants grow the next year from seeds.

biodiversity: the range of living things in an ecosystem.

biome: a large natural area with a distinctive climate, geology, and set of water resources. A biome's plants and animals are adapted for life there.

carnivore: an animal that eats only other animals.

climate: average weather patterns in an area over many years.

coniferous forest: a forest where most trees and bushes produce their seeds in cones and do not lose their leaves each year. Many have needles for leaves.

deciduous forest: a forest where most trees and bushes shed their leaves at the end of the growing season.

ecological community: the relationship between living things and their environment.

ecosystem: a community of living and nonliving things and their environment. Living things are plants, animals and insects. Nonliving things are soil, rocks, and water.

environment: everything in nature, living and nonliving.

erosion: when land is worn away by wind or water.

Glossary

extinct: the species has completely died out. It has disappeared from the planet.

glacier: an enormous mass of frozen snow and ice that moves across the earth's surface.

food chain: a community of animals and plants where each is eaten by another higher up in the chain.

geological events: earthquakes, eruptions of volcanoes, and erosion.

geology: the rocks, minerals, and physical structure of an area.

habitat: a plant or animal's home.

herbivore: an animal that eats only plants.

hibernate: to sleep through the winter.

migrate: to move from one environment to another when seasons or conditions change.

perennials: plants that live for more than one season.

plates: huge moving pieces of the earth's crust.

predator: an animal that hunts another animal for food.

prey: an animal hunted by a predator for food.

species: a type of animal or plant.

succulent: a plant with thick leaves that can store water.

treeline: as far up a mountain as trees can grow.

tundra: a vast region in the Arctic without trees. The soil below the top layer is always frozen.

Further Investigations

Cherry, Lynn. *How We Know What We Know About Our Changing Climate: Scientists and Kids Explore Global Warming.* Dawn Publications, 2008.

Latham, Donna. *Amazing Biome Projects You Can Build Yourself.* Nomad Press, 2009.

Reilly, Kathleen M. *Planet Earth: 25 Environmental Projects You Can Build Yourself.* Nomad Press, 2008.

Rothschild, David. *Earth Matters: An Encyclopedia of Ecology.* DK Publishing, 2008.

Smithsonian Institution National Museum of Natural History
www.mnh.si.edu
Washington, D.C.

US National Parks www.us-parks.com

Enchanted Learning, Biomes
www.enchantedlearning.com/biomes

Energy Efficiency and Renewable Energy
www.eere.energy.gov/kids

Geography for Kids www.kidsgeo.com

Inch in a Pinch: Saving the Earth
www.inchinapinch.com

Kids Do Ecology
www.kids.nceas.ucsb.edu

Library ThinkQuest
www.thinkquest.org

National Geographic Kids
www.kids.nationalgeographic.com

NOAA for Kids
www.oceanservice.noaa.gov/kids

Oceans for Youth
www.oceansforyouth.org

The Nature Conservancy
www.nature.org

World Wildlife Federation
www.panda.org

Index